To
_____

From
_____

_____

> "All the earth will worship thee, and shall sing unto thee; they shall sing to thy name."
>
> Selah.

The Power of Worship

"WORSHIP - "

An Unwavering Commitment Beyond Choice."

Dr. Letitia McPherson

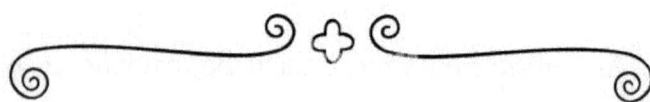

What is the outcome then? I will pray with the spirit and I will pray with the mind also; I will sing with the spirit and I will sing with the mind also.

1 Corinthians 14 :15

by God's Grace i Stand
PUBLISHER

The Power of Worship

Copyright © 2025 by Dr. Letitia McPherson
All rights reserved.

No part of this publication may be reproduced, distributed, or transmitted in any form or by any means, including photocopying, recording, or other electronic or mechanical methods, without the prior written permission of the publisher, except in the case of brief quotations embodied in critical reviews and certain other noncommercial uses permitted by copyright law.

*Scripture quotations are taken from the KJV and the NIV Translation * of the Bible, unless otherwise noted, and are used by permission. All rights reserved.*

For permission requests, write to the publisher at:
Dr. Letitia McPherson
bishopmcpherson@gmail.com
based in North York, Ontario Canada
978-1-990266-71-3
Printed in the USA by Amazon

Other Books by Dr. Letitia McPherson

The Power Series:

The Power of Forgiveness

The Power of Faith

The Power of Prayer

The Power of Worship

The Power of Grace

By God's Grace I Stand (Best Seller)

From the Mouth of the Prophet

Facing the Storms of Life

Walking Through the Valley

The Potter, The Clay, the Process

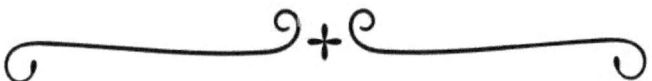

"Worship is not just a song; it's the anthem of a surrendered heart, the weapon of a weary soul, and the bridge that connects heaven to earth. In worship, we find God's presence, His power, and His peace."

Dr. Letitia McPherson

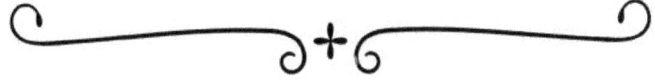

TABLE OF CONTENTS

Dedication 1

Preface 3

Introduction 7

Chapter 1: The Foundation of Worship 13

Chapter 2: The Heart of Worship 19

Chapter 3: Worship in the Storm 27

Chapter 4: A Heart Aligned with Heaven 35

Chapter 5: The Transformative Power of Worship 43

Chapter 6: Worship as a Spiritual Weapon 51

Chapter 7: Persistent Worship 59

Chapter 8: Worship in the Waiting	65
Chapter 9: Living a Life of Worship	73
Chapter 10: Why Do We Worship God?	81
Chapter 11: Worship That Echoes in Eternity	87
Conclusion	93

Dedication

To Pastor Ann Marie Morris and the Citadel Worship Team,

As your Bishop, I am deeply honored to serve alongside you in the ministry of worship. Your steadfast dedication, passion, and anointing as a worship leader have been a continual source of inspiration, not only to me but to everyone you lead into the presence of God. Week after week, you guide us with such humility and grace, creating an atmosphere where hearts are lifted, and heaven meets earth.

To you and your incredible team, thank you for your faithfulness, for your unity, and for the sacrifices you make to ensure that every note sung, every instrument played, and every moment of worship is an offering unto the Lord. You are more than musicians and singers; you are worshippers whose lives reflect the beauty of surrender to God.

This book is a celebration of worship and its transformative power—something we have witnessed together time and time again. May it serve as a testament to the incredible ways God moves through those who pour themselves out in worship.

With much gratitude and love,
Bishop

PREFACE

Worship has been the cornerstone of my life, a guiding force that has shaped my spiritual journey over the past fifty years. It is through worship that I have found strength in moments of weakness, clarity in times of confusion, and a deep connection with the heart of God that has carried me through every season of life. In the early days of my Christian walk, under the mentorship of my spiritual father, Pastor Paul Melnichuck of the Toronto Prayer Palace, I learned the art and significance of worship. Pastor Melnichuck, who recently transitioned to glory, instilled in me the truth that worship is not merely a Sunday activity—it is a lifestyle, a posture of the heart that invites heaven to meet earth.

Through worship, I have experienced countless miracles and moments of divine breakthrough. From witnessing unexplainable healings to finding peace during life's most chaotic storms, worship has continually proven to be a channel for God's miraculous power. I recall one specific instance when, amidst a dire situation, the simple act of worship opened doors to unexpected solutions, reaffirming that God's presence transforms not just the heart but also the circumstances around us.

I've seen God move powerfully during corporate worship and in the quiet, intimate moments of personal praise. One unforgettable testimony is the time I worshiped through a stroke. The medical professionals were astounded that I hadn't suffered severe damage, attributing it to the motion and focus that worship had brought during that episode. In reality, it was God's sustaining hand, reminding me that worship is more than a song; it is a lifeline.

This book is born out of a desire to share my experience of the transformative power of worship. It's an exploration of its depth and significance, blending scriptural teaching, personal testimonies, and practical insights to encourage you in your own worship journey. Worship is more than music; it's an act of surrender, a declaration of faith, and a pathway to encountering the presence of God.

Whether you're new to the faith or a seasoned believer, I pray this book will inspire you to cultivate a lifestyle of worship that draws you closer to the heart of God. May it challenge you to worship in spirit and in truth, to find strength in praise during trials, and to experience the joy of

God's presence in every season of life.

Let's embark on this journey together, exploring the power, purpose, and privilege of worship. My prayer is that you will discover, as I have, that worship changes everything—not just our circumstances but our very hearts.

Dr. Letitia McPherson

INTRODUCTION
The Power of Worship

"Holy, holy, holy is the Lord Almighty;
the whole earth is full of His glory."

Isaiah 6:3

Worship is one of the most profound ways we connect with God. It is both an invitation and a response—an invitation to step into His presence and a response to His goodness and majesty. Worship aligns our hearts with heaven, reshaping the way we see God and ourselves. It allows us to view His majesty and love with fresh clarity, transforming our perspective from one of limitation to one of divine possibility. Just as a mirror reflects light, worship reflects God's glory back to Him and illuminates our true identity as His children. It is in worship that we begin to grasp the majesty of who He is and the immense love He has for us as His children. For example, during a particularly difficult season in my life, worship became my anchor. As I lifted my voice in praise, scriptures like Isaiah 6:3—'Holy, holy, holy is the Lord Almighty; the whole earth is full of His glory'—came alive in my spirit, reminding me of His sovereignty and faithfulness. Worship doesn't just align us with heaven; it aligns us with God's purpose, renewing our hope and igniting our faith.

Acts 16:25-26 provides a vivid illustration of the power of worship in action. Picture Paul and Silas, beaten and imprisoned, yet choosing to sing hymns and pray to God. Their voices, echoing through the dark prison walls, reflected unshakable faith. Suddenly, an earthquake shook the foundations of the prison, breaking their chains and flinging open the doors. This miraculous moment didn't just set them free; it left the other prisoners and even the jailer in awe, ultimately leading the jailer and his family to salvation.

This story beautifully demonstrates that worship transcends our circumstances, becoming a conduit for God's power and glory to manifest. Paul and Silas, beaten and imprisoned, chose to worship in their darkest hour, an act of unshakable faith and profound courage. Despite their pain and chains, they lifted their voices in hymns and prayers, transforming their prison cell into a sanctuary of hope and praise. This remarkable decision not only defied their circumstances but also demonstrated the unparalleled power of worship to bring light into the darkest places of life. As they sang hymns and prayed, an earthquake shook the prison, breaking their chains and opening the doors. Their worship not only brought their own deliverance but also impacted the prisoners and the jailer. This story reminds us that worship is not dependent on our circumstances; it's an act of faith that ushers in God's presence and power.

For me, worship has been a source of strength, healing, and transformation. I remember a time when I faced one of the most trying seasons of my life. The weight of ministry challenges and personal struggles felt unbearable. During that period, I found solace in the simple act of lifting my voice in worship. One night, I sang "The Goodness of God" over and over again, and as I did, the peace of the Holy Spirit washed over me. It was in those moments of worship that my heart found healing and my spirit was renewed, reminding me that God's goodness never fails. It's where I've found peace in the midst of storms and clarity in times of confusion. Worship is not about performance or perfection; it's about connection. I remember many of our Sunday services when the worship team led with such authenticity that the entire congregation felt the tangible presence of God. It wasn't about hitting the right notes or having a flawless performance; it was about hearts fully surrendered to Him. Worship, in its truest form, is about drawing near to God, offering Him our love and devotion, and experiencing His presence in return. It's about recognizing God's worthiness and offering Him our hearts, no matter what season of life we're in.

This book is a journey through the many facets of worship—from its biblical foundation and spiritual power to its ability to transform lives and draw us closer to God. We'll explore its biblical foundation, its role in spiritual warfare, and its power to bring breakthrough and transformation. Along the way, I'll share personal stories of how worship has shaped my life and ministry, including miraculous testimonies that testify to the greatness of our God.

As you read these pages, I pray that your understanding of worship will deepen and that your heart will be stirred to pursue God with greater passion. Worship is not confined to a church building or a specific style of music; it's an open invitation for God's presence to permeate every moment of our lives. Whether in the quiet solitude of morning prayer, the bustle of daily tasks, or the collective praise of a congregation, worship creates space for divine connection and transformation. It's my hope that this book will inspire you to live a life of worship—a life that reflects the glory of the One who is worthy of it all.

Chapter 1

The Foundation of Worship

I beseech you therefore, brethren, by the mercies of God, that you present your bodies a living sacrifice, holy, acceptable to God, which is your reasonable service.

Romans 12:1

Worship is more than songs and melodies; it is a weapon, a declaration of faith, and a surrender to God's sovereignty. Psalm 22:3 tells us, "Yet You are holy, enthroned on the praises of Israel." When we worship, we create a dwelling place for God's presence. And where His presence is, miracles happen, chains are broken, and lives are transformed.

In my early days as a believer, I learned the foundational truths about worship under the guidance of Pastor Paul Melnichuck. He taught me that worship is not confined to a Sunday service but is a lifestyle—a daily offering of our hearts to God. This understanding shaped the way I approached every aspect of my life. Worship became my refuge, my strength, and my connection to heaven.

One of the most striking examples of worship's power is found in the story of King Jehoshaphat in 2 Chronicles 20. When faced with a vast enemy army, Jehoshaphat appointed singers to lead his army in worship. As they sang and praised the Lord, God set ambushes against their enemies, and the battle was won without the Israelites lifting a single weapon. Worship was their strategy, and God's power was their victory.

Dr. Letitia McPherson

I have experienced similar breakthroughs through worship in my own life. I remember a time when I faced overwhelming financial strain in ministry. The situation seemed impossible, and I was tempted to despair. Instead, I gathered my team, and we spent hours in worship, lifting our voices and hearts to God. Miraculously, within days, an unexpected donation arrived, covering the need entirely. Worship transformed a moment of desperation into an opportunity for God's provision.

Another powerful testimony of worship came during a critical health challenge. As I prepared for a significant medical procedure, anxiety threatened to overwhelm me. But the Holy Spirit impressed upon my heart to sing the worship song, "The Goodness of God." As I sang, a supernatural peace enveloped me, fulfilling the promise of Philippians

4:7: "And the peace of God, which transcends all understanding, will guard your hearts and your minds in Christ Jesus." Even the medical staff noticed the calmness I carried, a testimony to the sustaining power of worship.

Worship is not just about what we offer to God; it's a divine exchange where He shapes, renews, and transforms us. Isaiah 61:3 captures this beautifully: "to bestow on them a crown of beauty instead of ashes, the oil of joy instead of mourning, and a garment of praise instead of a spirit of despair." Worship aligns our hearts with God's purposes, builds our faith, and enables us to live out His will in our daily lives. It is not limited to singing but encompasses every aspect of our existence, as Romans 12:1 urges us to "offer your bodies as a living sacrifice, holy and pleasing to God—this is your true and proper worship."

In this chapter, we've explored the biblical foundations of worship, its transformative role, and its ability to bring breakthrough in our lives. Worship invites us into God's presence, declaring His sovereignty and aligning our hearts with His will. It is not just something we do; it is who we are called to be.

As we conclude this chapter, I invite you to reflect on your own worship journey. What does worship mean to you? How can you create space in your life for God's presence to dwell? Worship is an invitation to experience the fullness of God's power and love. Let it become the foundation of your life, shaping your thoughts, guiding your actions, and transforming your heart.

CHAPTER 2

The Heart of Worship

"Delight yourself in the Lord, and He will give you the desires of your heart."

Psalm 37:4

Worship begins in the heart. It is more than a melody sung or a ritual performed; it is the overflow of a heart that is fully devoted to God. Jesus said in John 4:23, "But the hour is coming, and is now here, when the true worshipers will worship the Father in spirit and truth, for the Father is seeking such people to worship Him." This verse reminds us that God is not looking for outward expressions alone but for hearts that are aligned with His.

In my own journey, I've learned that worship is about relationship. It's about intimacy with God—a deep connection that goes beyond words. Worship draws us closer to His heart, and in His presence, we are changed. The closer we draw to Him, the more our desires align with His will. Worship is the means by which we surrender our own agendas and invite God to reign in our lives.

One of the most transformative lessons about worship came to me early in my Christian walk. I vividly remember a worship service where the music paused, and the pastor encouraged everyone to worship in their own words. At first, I felt awkward, unsure of what to say or do. But as I closed my eyes and began to focus on God's goodness, words of love and gratitude began to flow from my heart. In that moment, I experienced the essence of worship—a personal connection with God that words cannot fully describe.

The heart of worship is also about humility. It's about recognizing who God is and who we are in light of Him. Isaiah 6:1-5 provides a profound example of this. When Isaiah saw the Lord seated on His throne, high and lifted up, his immediate response was humility and repentance: "Woe to me!" he cried. "I am ruined! For I am a man of unclean lips, and I live among a people of unclean lips, and my eyes have seen the King, the Lord Almighty." True worship brings us to our knees, reminding us of our need for God's mercy and grace.

Another key aspect of the heart of worship is gratitude. 1 Thessalonians 5:16-18 instructs us to "rejoice always, pray continually, give thanks in all circumstances; for this is God's will for you in Christ Jesus." Gratitude shifts our perspective, allowing us to see God's hand in every situation. Even in difficult times, a heart of gratitude turns our focus from our challenges to His faithfulness. I've often found that when I choose to thank God in the midst of trials, my heart begins to shift. Gratitude unlocks joy and brings us into a deeper awareness of His presence.

Let me share another example from my life. There was a season when I faced immense challenges in ministry. Discouragement weighed heavily on me, and I struggled to find the strength to continue. One morning during my quiet time, I felt the Holy Spirit prompt me to spend that time in worship instead of bringing my usual list of prayer requests. I began to sing "Great Is Thy Faithfulness," and as I sang, something shifted in my spirit. My focus moved from the obstacles before me to the greatness of God. By the end of that worship session, I felt a renewed sense of hope and purpose. The challenges didn't disappear, but my heart was transformed, and I knew that God was in control.

Scripture is filled with examples of worship flowing from grateful hearts. Consider David, a man after God's own heart, who wrote countless psalms of worship. In Psalm 103:1-2, he declares, "Bless the Lord, O my soul, and all that is within me, bless His holy name! Bless the Lord, O my soul, and forget not all His benefits." David's worship was rooted in a deep awareness of God's goodness and faithfulness.

To cultivate the heart of worship, we must make it a daily practice. Here are a few ways to do so:

1. **Spend Time in God's Word:** Worship

begins with knowing who God is, and the Bible reveals His character and promises.

2. **Practice Gratitude:** Make a habit of thanking God for His blessings, both big and small.

3. **Create Space for Worship:** Set aside time each day to worship God through song, prayer, or quiet reflection.

4. **Surrender Daily:** Begin each day by surrendering your plans, desires, and worries to God, inviting Him to lead.

As we align our hearts with God's, our worship becomes a natural response to His goodness and grace. It's not about perfection but about connection. Worship flows from hearts that are fully devoted to Him, and it transforms every aspect of our lives. As Psalm 37:4 reminds us, "Delight yourself in the Lord, and He will give you the desires of your heart." When we delight in Him, our desires begin to reflect His will, and our lives become a living testimony of His glory.

Now! let me ask you: How is your heart aligned with God's today? Take a moment to reflect and invite Him to shape your heart into one that overflows with worship. Let the heart of worship become the rhythm of your life, drawing you closer to Him and transforming you from the inside out.

CHAPTER 3

Worship in the Storm

*"I sought the LORD, and he heard me,
and delivered me from all my fears"*

Psalm 34:4

Life is full of storms—unexpected challenges, heartbreaking losses, and seasons of uncertainty that test the very core of our faith. Yet, worship has the power to anchor us during these turbulent times. It redirects our focus from the storm to the One who holds it all in His hands. Worshiping in the storm is not about denying our pain or pretending everything is fine; it is about declaring God's goodness and sovereignty in the midst of it.

In Acts 16:25-26, we see this vividly demonstrated in the lives of Paul and Silas. Beaten, shackled, and imprisoned, they chose to worship God. "About midnight, Paul and Silas were praying and singing hymns to God, and the prisoners were listening to them. Suddenly, there was such a violent earthquake that the foundations of the prison were shaken. At once, all the prison doors flew open, and everyone's chains came loose." Their worship didn't just change their circumstances; it changed the atmosphere. Their faith-filled praise shook the foundations of the prison, opening doors and breaking chains—not only for themselves but for everyone around them.

Dr. Letitia McPherson

Worship as an Act of Defiance

Worship in the storm is an act of defiance against fear, doubt, and despair. It is a declaration that God is greater than our circumstances. When we lift our voices in praise during difficult times, we are saying, "Lord, I trust You. I may not understand what is happening, but I know You are faithful, and I believe You are working all things together for my good" (Romans 8:28).

There was a time in my life when I experienced this firsthand. I faced a health crisis—a stroke that could have left me unable to function. The doctors told me that I needed to stay in motion, but what they didn't realize was that my "motion" was worship. In the midst of that terrifying experience, I lifted my hands, sang songs of praise, and declared God's healing over my body. I worshiped through the pain, the fear, and the uncertainty. And God met me in that place. He not only brought me through the storm but also strengthened my faith in ways I could never have imagined.

The Perspective of Worship

Worship shifts our perspective. It reminds us that God is bigger than our problems and that His power is greater than anything we face. In Isaiah 61:3, we are promised "a garment of praise instead of a spirit of despair." When we choose to worship, we put on that garment of praise, allowing God to lift the weight of despair from our shoulders.

King Jehoshaphat experienced this in 2 Chronicles 20 when faced with a vast army coming against Judah. Instead of panicking, he sought the Lord and led his people in worship. The worshipers went ahead of the army, singing, "Give thanks to the Lord, for His love endures forever." As they praised, God caused their enemies to turn on one another, and victory was won without a single weapon being drawn. Worship not only changes our perspective but also activates God's power on our behalf.

Worship as a Testimony

When we worship in the storm, it becomes a testimony to those around us. Just as Paul and Silas's worship impacted the prisoners, our praise can inspire faith in others. People notice when we choose to worship in the face of adversity. They see the peace, strength, and hope that come from trusting in God, and it points them to Him.

I remember a time when my worship became a testimony. During a difficult season in ministry, I stood before the congregation and led them in praise, even though my heart was heavy. After the service, someone approached me and said, "Seeing you worship today gave me the strength to keep going." I realized then that our worship is not just for us; it has the power to encourage and uplift those around us.

Practical Steps for Worshiping in the Storm

1. **Acknowledge Your Feelings:** It's okay to be honest with God about your pain, fear, or frustration. David often poured out his heart in the Psalms, expressing his struggles while still declaring God's faithfulness.

2. **Choose Praise:** Worship is a choice. Even when you don't feel like it, begin to praise God for who He is. Declare His goodness, His promises, and His faithfulness.

3. **Use Scripture:** Find verses that speak to your situation and turn them into prayers

and songs of worship. For example, if you're facing fear, declare Psalm 34:4: "I sought the Lord, and He answered me; He delivered me from all my fears."

4. **Surround Yourself with Worship:** Play worship music in your home, car, or workplace. Let it fill the atmosphere and remind you of God's presence.

5. **Invite Others to Join You:** Sometimes, the storm feels too heavy to face alone. Reach out to trusted friends or fellow believers and worship together. There is strength in unity.

Reflection Questions:

1. Can you think of a time when worship carried you through a difficult season? What did you learn about God in that experience?

2. How can you incorporate worship into your

life when you're facing challenges?

3. Who might be encouraged by your decision to worship in the storm?

Call to Action:

This week, take time to worship God in the midst of whatever you're facing. Choose a song that declares His faithfulness and sing it out, even if your circumstances haven't changed yet. Trust that as you worship, God is working behind the scenes, and His power is being unleashed in your life.

In the storms of life, let worship be your anchor. Let it remind you that the same God who calmed the storm for His disciples and parted the Red Sea for Moses is with you now. Worship is not just a response to what God has done; it is an act of faith in what He will do. Keep worshiping, keep trusting, and watch as God's presence transforms your storm into a testimony.

CHAPTER 4

A Heart Aligned with Heaven

For My thoughts are not your thoughts,
Nor are your ways My ways," says the Lord.
"For as the heavens are higher than the earth, So
are My ways higher than your ways, And My
thoughts than your thoughts.

Isaiah 55:8-9

Worship is more than an act; it is the posture of our hearts, a reflection of our innermost devotion to God. A heart aligned with heaven doesn't just sing or lift hands in praise—it beats in rhythm with God's will, rejoicing in His presence and surrendering to His purposes. Worship begins and thrives in the heart that seeks Him earnestly.

One of the clearest expressions of this truth is found in Matthew 22:37, where Jesus declares, "Love the Lord your God with all your heart and with all your soul and with all your mind." Worship flows out of this love. It's a natural response to knowing God and understanding who He is. But how do we cultivate a heart that is truly aligned with heaven?

Cultivating a Heart of Worship

Alignment with heaven begins with surrender. It's laying down our desires, our fears, and even our plans, trusting that God's ways are higher than ours (Isaiah 55:8-9). Surrender doesn't come easily, especially when life feels uncertain or when our own will seems so strong. Yet, true worship starts when we say, "Not my will, but Yours be done" (Luke 22:42).

In my own life, I have often wrestled with this kind of surrender. One vivid moment came when I was faced with a major decision regarding ministry. I was torn between two options, each with its own set of challenges and opportunities. As I prayed and worshiped, the words of the hymn "I Surrender All" came to mind. Singing those words became my act of surrender, and in that moment, I felt God's peace envelop me. The path forward became clear, not because my circumstances changed, but because my heart aligned with His will.

Another essential element of a heart aligned with heaven is humility. Psalm 51:17 reminds us, "The sacrifices of God are a broken spirit; a broken and contrite heart, O God, you will not despise." Humility in worship is about recognizing who God is and who we are in relation to Him. It's acknowledging our dependence on His grace and mercy. When our hearts are humble, we can fully enter into the presence of God, unencumbered by pride or self-reliance.

The Transformative Power of Worship

Worship has a transformative effect on the heart. When we worship, we invite God to mold and shape us. Romans 12:1 urges us to "offer your bodies as a living sacrifice, holy and pleasing to God—this is your true and proper worship." This sacrifice isn't just about outward actions; it's about an inward transformation where our hearts become fully His.

Think about David, a man after God's own heart (Acts 13:22). David's life was far from perfect, but his heart was continually turned toward God.

Whether he was rejoicing in victory or repenting in brokenness, David's worship reflected a heart aligned with heaven. In Psalm 139:23-24, he prays, "Search me, God, and know my heart; test me and know my anxious thoughts. See if there is any offensive way in me, and lead me in the way everlasting." This willingness to be examined and refined is a hallmark of a worshipful heart.

Worship as a Daily Practice

Alignment with heaven is not a one-time event; it's a daily choice. Every day, we have the opportunity to set our hearts on God through worship. This doesn't mean we have to spend hours singing hymns or praying—though those are beautiful expressions of worship. It means living with an awareness of His presence and responding to Him in gratitude and obedience.

The Power of Worship

One practical way to cultivate this daily alignment is through intentional moments of worship. Start your day with a simple prayer of gratitude, acknowledging God's goodness. Reflect on His promises throughout the day, letting Scripture guide your thoughts and actions. And as you end your day, take a moment to thank Him for His faithfulness.

Another way to nurture a worshipful heart is by surrounding yourself with reminders of God's presence. Whether it's worship music playing in your home, a favorite verse displayed where you can see it, or a journal where you record answered prayers, these reminders help keep your heart focused on Him.

Reflection Questions:

1. In what areas of your life do you need to surrender to God's will?

2. How can you cultivate humility in your worship?

3. What practical steps can you take to make worship a daily practice?

Call to Action:

This week, spend time reflecting on your heart's alignment with God. Ask Him to reveal any areas that need surrender or refinement. As you worship, invite Him to transform your heart, aligning it with His will and purposes.

True worship begins in the heart, and a heart aligned with heaven reflects the beauty, love, and sovereignty of God. Let your worship not only glorify Him but also draw you closer to His heart, transforming you into the person He created you to be.

CHAPTER 5

The Transformative Power of Worship

I beseech you, therefore, brethren, by the mercies of God, that you present your bodies a living sacrifice, holy, acceptable to God, which is your reasonable service.

Romans 12:1

Worship has the power to transform—not just our circumstances but also our hearts, minds, and lives. It is an encounter with the living God that leaves us forever changed. As we offer ourselves in worship, something supernatural happens: chains are broken, perspectives are shifted, and we step into the fullness of who God created us to be.

The Apostle Paul reminds us in Romans 12:1, "Therefore, I urge you, brothers and sisters, in view of God's mercy, to offer your bodies as a living sacrifice, holy and pleasing to God—this is your true and proper worship." Worship is not limited to a Sunday service or a favorite song; it is a lifestyle of surrender and devotion. When we align our hearts with Heaven, we position ourselves to be transformed by the One who makes all things new.

Worship Transforms Our Perspective

Life's trials can weigh heavily on our hearts, leaving us feeling defeated and hopeless. Yet, when we worship, our focus shifts from our problems to God's power. Worship elevates us above our circumstances, reminding us that He is greater than any challenge we face.

I remember a particular season when I felt overwhelmed by a health crisis. The weight of uncertainty was heavy, and fear threatened to consume me. But in the midst of that storm, I chose to worship. I didn't feel like it at first, but as I began to lift my voice in praise, something miraculous happened. The fear that once gripped me gave way to peace. I was reminded of Isaiah 26:3, "You will keep in perfect peace those whose minds are steadfast because they trust in You." Worship doesn't always change our circumstances immediately, but it changes us. It aligns our hearts with God's truth, enabling us to walk through the storm with faith and courage.

Worship Breaks Chains and Brings Freedom

The story of Paul and Silas in Acts 16 is a powerful example of the freedom that worship brings. Beaten and imprisoned, they could have chosen despair. Instead, they chose worship. At midnight, as they prayed and sang hymns, the prison walls shook, the chains fell off, and the doors flung open. Their worship not only set them free but also impacted everyone around them.

I'll never forget the day I faced carotid surgery. The weight of it all—my age, the risks, the uncertainty—left me feeling deeply anxious. But as I lay on the operating table, being prepped for anesthesia, the Holy Spirit gently nudged me to sing the worship song, "The Goodness of God." At first, I hesitated, but then I began to softly sing, "All my life You have been faithful, all my life You have been so, so good…." As the words flowed from my lips, something extraordinary happened. A wave of peace, unlike anything I had ever known, enveloped me. It was as though God Himself was in the room, reminding me of His faithfulness and goodness. In that moment, my fears melted away, and I felt completely surrendered to His will. That simple act of worship transformed my anxiety into confidence and trust, assuring me that God was in control.

The words of Psalm 16:11 came alive in my heart: "You make known to me the path of life; in Your presence there is fullness of joy; at Your right hand are pleasures forevermore." Truly, worship ushers us into God's presence, where His peace replaces fear, and His joy strengthens our hearts.

Worship Renews Our Identity

One of the most profound transformations that occurs in worship is the renewal of our identity. In worship, we are reminded that we are children of God, deeply loved and valued. The enemy often attacks our sense of worth, whispering lies that we are not enough or that we've failed too many times. But in the presence of God, those lies lose their power.

2 Corinthians 3:18 tells us, "And we all, who with unveiled faces contemplate the Lord's glory, are being transformed into His image with ever-increasing glory, which comes from the Lord, who is the Spirit." Worship allows us to see ourselves as God sees us—fearfully and wonderfully made, chosen, and redeemed.

Practical Steps to Experience Transformative Worship

1. Be Intentional: Create space in your daily life for worship. Whether through music, prayer, or reading Scripture, dedicate time to focus on God.

2. Engage Fully: Worship with your whole

heart, mind, and body. Lift your hands, sing loudly, or kneel in reverence. Let your worship be an outward expression of your inner surrender.

3. Use Scripture in Worship: Declare God's promises as part of your worship. For example, you can pray and sing verses like Psalm 34:1, "I will bless the Lord at all times; His praise shall continually be in my mouth."

4. Invite Others to Worship: Worshiping in community amplifies its impact. As Matthew 18:20 says, "For where two or three gather in My name, there am I with them."

The Ongoing Transformation

The beauty of worship is that its transformative power is ongoing. Each time we enter God's presence, we are renewed and strengthened. Worship not only fills us with joy but also equips us to face life's challenges with confidence in God's faithfulness.

As we close this chapter, remember that worship is an invitation to draw closer to God. It is a powerful exchange where we offer our praise, and He meets us with His presence. Through worship, we are transformed from the inside out, becoming more like Christ and stepping into the abundant life He has promised.

So, let us worship with boldness and expectation, knowing that every time we lift our voices, we are unleashing the transformative power of Heaven on earth.

CHAPTER 6

Worship as a Spiritual Weapon

He who dwells in the secret place of the Most High

Shall abide under the shadow of the Almighty.

I will say of the Lord, "He is my refuge and my

fortress; My God, in Him I will trust."

Psalm 91:1-2

Have you ever thought about worship as more than just an expression of love for God? Worship is a spiritual weapon—a divine strategy given to us by the Almighty to stand against the forces of darkness. It's not merely a melody sung or words spoken; it's an act of warfare that shifts atmospheres, dismantles strongholds, and declares the ultimate authority of our King. Worship is how we fight battles that cannot be seen with the naked eye.

Paul reminds us of this unseen reality in Ephesians 6:12: "For we wrestle not against flesh and blood, but against principalities, against powers, against the rulers of the darkness of this world, against spiritual wickedness in high places." The challenges we encounter in life—a failing health diagnosis, a wayward child, or an overwhelming financial crisis—are often more than physical or emotional struggles. They represent a spiritual conflict that demands spiritual tools. And worship is one of the most potent tools we have.

Worship aligns us with heaven's purposes. It shifts the focus from our problems to God's promises. When we lift our hands in surrender and our voices in praise, we are not ignoring the reality of our struggles; we are acknowledging the greater reality of God's sovereignty. Worship is a declaration of faith that God is greater than any challenge we face, and in that declaration lies tremendous power.

Let me share a personal moment when worship became my weapon. During one of the most difficult seasons in my ministry, opposition arose on every side. It felt like the weight of discouragement was crushing me. One evening, I retreated to my prayer room, but I couldn't find the words to pray. So, I began to sing. I didn't ask God for anything; I simply lifted my voice in worship. The song "You Are My Strength" became my anthem, and as I sang, I felt a shift in the atmosphere. The fear and heaviness that had gripped my heart began to melt away, replaced by an overwhelming sense of peace and assurance. It was as though God wrapped me in

The Power of Worship

His arms, reminding me, "I've got you." The challenges didn't disappear overnight, but my heart was strengthened, and my resolve was renewed.

The Bible gives us profound examples of worship as a weapon. In 2 Chronicles 20, when Judah faced an overwhelming enemy, King Jehoshaphat placed worshippers at the front lines of the battle. As they sang and praised God, the Lord Himself set ambushes against their enemies, leading Judah to victory without lifting a single sword. Their worship not only brought God's intervention but also confounded their adversaries. This story reminds us that worship does what human strategies cannot—it invites divine intervention.

Worship doesn't just confuse the enemy; it fortifies us. Psalm 91:1-2 promises, "Whoever dwells in the shelter of the Most High will rest in the shadow of the Almighty. I will say of the Lord,

'He is my refuge and my fortress, my God, in whom I trust.'" Worship brings us under the shadow of God's presence, where we are shielded from the fiery darts of the enemy. In worship, we declare that the enemy has no hold over us because we stand under the authority and protection of the King of Kings.

Sometimes, worship is the loud shout of victory, like the Israelites circling the walls of Jericho (Joshua 6:20). Other times, it's the whispered prayer of a heart that can barely find the strength to believe. But in every form, worship is powerful because it is rooted in faith. It is faith that says, "God, I trust You," even when the answer seems delayed or the battle seems lost.

As you face your own battles, I urge you to take up the weapon of worship. Play songs that remind you of God's greatness. Sing from the depths of your soul, even if your voice trembles. Declare His promises over your situation, as 2 Corinthians 10:4 reminds us, "The weapons of our warfare are not carnal, but mighty through God to the pulling down of strongholds." Your worship can dismantle strongholds, bring peace to chaos, and pave the way for God's miracles.

In your darkest moments, let worship be your light. When fear whispers that you are defeated, let worship roar that you are victorious. When doubt creeps in, let worship remind you of who God is—a deliverer, a healer, a way-maker. Lift your hands, bow your knees, or simply sit in stillness as you offer your heart to Him. Every act of worship is a declaration of war against the enemy and a proclamation of trust in the One who has already won the victory.

Never underestimate the power of your

Dr. Letitia McPherson

worship. It's not just a song; it's a strategy. It's not just an expression; it's an encounter with the living God. So, worship boldly, worship persistently, and watch as God fights for you.

CHAPTER 7

Persistent Worship

But I will sing of Your power; Yes, I will sing aloud of Your mercy in the morning; For You have been my defense And refuge in the day of my trouble.

Psalm 59:16

Worship is not a one-time act; it's a lifestyle. It's easy to worship when life is going well, but what about when the answers don't come, or the storm seems never-ending? Persistent worship is the key to unlocking doors that seem permanently shut and breaking chains that feel unyielding. It's worship that says, "Even if I don't see it now, I trust

You, God."

Jesus shared the parable of the persistent widow in Luke 18:1-8 to teach us about the power of persistence in prayer and worship. The widow, despite being denied justice repeatedly, kept coming to the judge until he granted her request. Jesus used this story to remind us that persistence pays off—not because we wear God down, but because it demonstrates our faith and trust in His timing and will.

I remember a season when I was praying for healing in my family. It was a time of emotional exhaustion and spiritual testing. I would sit at the piano and sing "Way Maker" over and over again. Even when the healing didn't come right away, the words reminded me that God was working, even when I couldn't see it. Day after day, I worshipped, declaring that He is a miracle worker and a promise keeper. Looking back now, I see how God used that time of waiting to deepen my faith and prepare my heart for the testimony that would come.

Persistent worship keeps us anchored. Psalm 40:1-3 says, "I waited patiently for the Lord; he turned to me and heard my cry. He lifted me out of the slimy pit, out of the mud and mire; he set my feet on a rock and gave me a firm place to stand. He put a new song in my mouth, a hymn of praise to our God." Waiting on God can be hard, but worship during the waiting brings us closer to Him and fills our hearts with hope.

Let's not forget Paul and Silas, who worshipped in a dark prison cell. Their worship wasn't contingent on their freedom; it was an act of faith in the midst of bondage. Their persistent worship brought an earthquake that broke their chains and opened prison doors (Acts 16:25-26). That same

The Power of Worship

power is available to us today.

Persistent worship is not just for the miraculous moments; it's for the mundane days, the seasons of waiting, and the times when hope feels distant. When you choose to worship despite the circumstances, you are declaring that God's promises are greater than your problems. Worship becomes your lifeline, connecting you to God's unchanging character and His unfailing love.

Practical Steps for Persistent Worship:

1. Create a Worship Playlist: Fill it with songs that lift your spirit and declare God's goodness (Psalm 59:16).

2. Set a Daily Worship Time: Even if it's just five minutes, make worship a consistent part of your day (Psalm 34:1).

3. Write a Worship Journal: Record moments

when God moves in your life through worship; revisit them during difficult times (Psalm 77:11-12).

4. Worship with Others: Join a worship group or invite friends to sing and pray with you. There is strength in unity (Matthew 18:20).

Persistent worship is a declaration that God is faithful, even in the waiting. It's a statement to the enemy that your faith cannot be shaken. So, when you feel too weak to pray, sing. When doubts creep in, speak God's promises out loud. Find songs that resonate with your spirit and let them carry you through. Worship boldly, and trust that God is working behind the scenes, even when you can't see it. Keep worshipping and watch how God moves in ways that exceed your expectations.

CHAPTER 8

Worship in the Waiting

My soul shall make its boast in the Lord;
The humble shall hear of it and be glad.
Oh, magnify the Lord with me, And
let us exalt His name together.

Psalm 34:2-3

Waiting is one of the most challenging aspects of life. Whether it's waiting for a breakthrough, an answered prayer, or clarity for the next step, the seasons of waiting can feel like endless stretches of uncertainty. Yet, it is in these moments that worship becomes not just a lifeline, but a powerful act of faith. Worship in the waiting is about trusting God's character when we cannot see His hand and praising Him for who He is rather than what He does.

Isaiah 40:31 gives us a profound promise: "But those who wait for the Lord shall renew their strength; they shall mount up with wings like eagles; they shall run and not be weary; they shall walk and not faint." This kind of waiting is not passive; it's an active posture of hope, faith, and worship. Through worship, we declare that we trust God to work all things together for good (Romans 8:28), even when we cannot yet see the outcome.

I'll never forget a deeply transformative experience during one of our Upper Room all-night worship services. At the time, the ministry was facing significant financial difficulties, and we desperately needed a breakthrough. While we prayed and sought God, the Holy Spirit impressed on us to continue worshipping and to wait on Him. It was not easy to quiet our anxious hearts, but we obeyed. The atmosphere shifted as we lifted our voices in praise, declaring His faithfulness even in the face of uncertainty. The next day, we witnessed a financial miracle from an entirely unexpected source—an answer so precise and timely that we could only attribute it to God. That experience taught me that worship in the waiting creates the space for God to move in miraculous ways.

The Bible is filled with stories of individuals who worshipped in the waiting and witnessed God's power. Consider the disciples in Acts 1, who were instructed by Jesus to wait in Jerusalem for the promised Holy Spirit. They didn't waste their waiting by succumbing to doubt or distraction; instead, they gathered together in prayer and worship. Ten days later, their waiting was rewarded at Pentecost when the Holy Spirit descended, empowering them to change the course of history (Acts 2). Their worship prepared them for the fulfillment of God's promise.

Another powerful example is found in the story of Hannah in 1 Samuel 1. Her longing for a child was met with years of waiting and unfulfilled prayers. Yet, in her pain, she worshipped. She poured out her heart to God in prayer, trusting that He saw her tears and heard her cries. Her waiting wasn't wasted, and in time, God blessed her with Samuel, who became one of the greatest prophets in Israel's history. Hannah's story reminds us that worship in the waiting is not about denying our pain—it's about offering it to God as an act of trust.

Worship during the waiting doesn't just change our circumstances; it transforms us. It aligns our hearts with God's purposes, builds our faith, and reminds us of His faithfulness. Lamentations 3:25 declares, "The Lord is good to those whose hope is in Him, to the one who seeks Him." Worship is an active declaration of hope—a statement to the enemy, and even to ourselves, that our trust is in God alone.

I experienced this transformation personally during a health scare that required carotid artery surgery. I was anxious about the procedure, given the risks and my age. The uncertainty was overwhelming, but as I was being prepped for anesthesia, the Holy Spirit nudged me to sing the worship song "The Goodness of God." As I sang, "All my life You have been faithful; all my life You have been so, so good," a profound peace washed over me. I knew in that moment that God was in control. The surgery went smoothly, and I came out of it with a renewed understanding of His presence in even the most vulnerable moments.

Worship in the waiting also shifts our focus from what we lack to the abundance of who God is. Psalm 34:3 invites us to "magnify the Lord" together, lifting our eyes from our circumstances to His greatness. This shift doesn't always change our situation immediately, but it changes us. It gives us the strength to endure, the faith to believe, and the peace to trust.

How to Worship in the Waiting

If you're in a season of waiting, here are some practical ways to turn your waiting into worship:

1. Create a Playlist of Faith:

Fill it with songs that remind you of God's promises and faithfulness. Let those melodies carry you through moments of doubt.

2. Speak the Scriptures:

Write down verses like Isaiah 40:31, Psalm 37:7, and Romans 8:28, and speak them over your life. Use them as declarations of trust in God's plan.

3. Journal Your Worship:

Write down your prayers, your praises, and even your frustrations. Offer them all to God as part of your worship.

4. Gather in Worship:

Surround yourself with others who will worship and wait with you. There's power in unity, as Jesus reminds us in Matthew 18:20: "For where two or three gather in My name, there am I with them."

5. Sing Through the Silence:

Even when it feels like nothing is happening, let worship be the bridge that carries you from despair to hope. Remember, waiting is not wasted when we worship. It becomes a sacred time where God refines us, draws us closer to Him, and prepares us for the blessings to come. So lift your voice, even in the uncertainty. Trust that the God who holds the universe also holds your future. Worship in the waiting, knowing that your song is moving the heart of heaven and setting the stage for your breakthrough.

CHAPTER 9

Living a Life of Worship

And whatever you do, do it heartily, as to the Lord and not to men, knowing that from the Lord you will receive the reward of the inheritance; for you serve the Lord Christ.

Colossians 3:23-24

What does it mean to live a life of worship? Is worship confined to the songs we sing on Sunday mornings or the quiet moments we spend in prayer? While these are beautiful expressions of worship, true worship extends far beyond the walls of a church building or the melodies of a hymn. Living a life of worship means offering every aspect of ourselves—our time, talents, resources, and even our struggles—as an act of devotion to God.

Romans 12:1 says it best: "Therefore, I urge you, brothers and sisters, in view of God's mercy, to offer your bodies as a living sacrifice, holy and pleasing to God—this is your true and proper worship." Worship is not just what we do with our voices; it's what we do with our lives. Every choice we make, every word we speak, and every action we take can be an offering of worship to our Creator.

I've seen this principle at work in my own life. I remember a particularly challenging season when I was juggling ministry responsibilities, family commitments, and personal health struggles. It felt impossible to balance everything, and I often wondered if I was truly honoring God in my busyness. One day, as I read Colossians 3:23—"Whatever you do, work at it with all your heart, as working for the Lord, not for human masters"—it hit me: even the small, seemingly mundane tasks of life could be acts of worship if done with the right heart. From that moment, I began to approach every responsibility as an opportunity to glorify God. Whether I was preparing a sermon, cooking dinner, or simply listening to a friend in need, I reminded myself that these acts, when done for Him, were sacred.

Gratitude as Worship

Living a life of worship starts with gratitude. Paul says it best in 1 Thessalonians 5:16-18: "Rejoice always, pray continually, give thanks in all circumstances; for this is God's will for you in Christ Jesus." Gratitude has an incredible way of shifting our focus. Instead of dwelling on what we don't have or what's going wrong, it helps us see what God is already doing. It reminds us of His faithfulness. Life isn't always easy, but even in the hard times, choosing gratitude doesn't just change our perspective; it lifts our hearts. It's like saying, "God, I see You in this. I trust You're working, even if I don't understand it yet."

Stewardship as Worship

Another vital aspect of living a life of worship is stewardship—how we handle what God has given us. This includes our money, talents, time, and even the opportunities that come our way. It's about recognizing that everything we have comes from God and asking, "How can I use this to honor You?"

For example, giving to someone in need or volunteering at church might seem small, but they're powerful acts of worship. Proverbs 3:9 says, "Honor the Lord with your wealth, with the firstfruits of all your crops." It's not just about money; it's about putting God first in everything and trusting Him with the rest. Stewardship means we approach every resource as a tool to bring glory to God and further His kingdom.

Worship in the Everyday

Here's the thing: worship isn't just about singing on Sundays. It's about how we live every single day. When we start to see worship as more than a moment or a ritual, everything changes. Washing dishes can become an act of gratitude. Helping a neighbor can be an expression of God's love. Even the most ordinary moments can be sacred when we invite God into them.

Psalm 34:3 invites us to "magnify the Lord"

together, lifting our eyes from our circumstances to His greatness. Worship as a lifestyle means saying, "God, I want You in every part of my life." When we do that, we begin to see Him in the little things—the conversations, the quiet moments, and the everyday tasks. That's where worship truly comes alive.

Practical Steps to Live a Life of Worship

1. **Start Your Day with Surrender:** Begin each morning by dedicating your day to God. Pray, "Lord, use me today for Your glory."

2. Be Present in the Moment: Recognize that every moment is an opportunity to worship—whether you're at work, at home, or with friends.

3. **Serve Others with Love:** Look for

opportunities to show Christ's love through acts of kindness and service.

4. **Cultivate Gratitude:** Keep a gratitude journal and thank God daily for His blessings.

5. **Reflect God's Character:** In every interaction, strive to reflect His love, patience, and grace.

Becoming True Worshipers

Living a life of worship doesn't mean life will always be easy or that we won't face challenges. But it does mean that we will carry a constant awareness of God's presence and a heart that seeks to honor Him in all we do. As John 4:23 reminds us, "Yet a time is coming and has now come when the true worshipers will worship the Father in the Spirit and in truth, for they are the kind of worshipers the

Father seeks."

May we strive to be those true worshipers, living each day as an act of devotion to the One who deserves our highest praise. Worship isn't just something we do; it's who we are. Let every breath, every step, and every moment be an offering of worship to our King.

CHAPTER 10

Why Do We Worship God?

Therefore, whether you eat or drink, or whatever you do, do all to the glory of God.

1 Corinthians 10:31

Why do we worship God? It's a question that often lingers in the hearts of both new believers and seasoned worshippers alike. Worship is such an integral part of our faith, yet understanding the "why" behind it can deepen its meaning and transform it from routine to revelation.

We worship God because of who He is. In

Revelation 4:11, the elders in heaven declare, "You are worthy, our Lord and God, to receive glory and honor and power, for You created all things, and by Your will they were created and have their being." God is the Creator of all things—the One who spoke the universe into existence and knit each of us together in our mother's womb (Psalm 139:13-14). His glory is unmatched, His power unsearchable, and His love immeasurable. Worship is our response to His infinite worth and majesty.

We worship because of what He has done. From the dawn of creation to this very moment, God's fingerprints are all over history—both in the grand story of redemption and in the intimate details of our own lives. He is the God who parted the Red Sea for Moses, delivered Daniel from the lion's den, and walked with Shadrach, Meshach, and Abednego through the fiery furnace. And He is the same God who sent His only Son, Jesus Christ, to die for our sins and rise again, offering us eternal life. As Psalm 103:2-4 says, "Praise the Lord, my soul, and forget not all His benefits—who forgives all your sins and heals all your diseases, who redeems your life from the pit and crowns you with love and compassion."

But worship is more than thanksgiving for what God has done—it's an act of surrender to what He will do. Even when the future is unclear, we worship because we trust His character. He is faithful, good, and unchanging. Hebrews 13:8 reminds us, "Jesus Christ is the same yesterday and today and forever." Worship allows us to say, "Lord, I trust You with my tomorrow, because I've seen Your faithfulness in my yesterday."

We also worship because it is what we were created to do. Isaiah 43:7 says, "Everyone who is called by My name, whom I created for My glory, whom I formed and made." Worship is not just

The Power of Worship

something we do; it's who we are. We are worshippers by design, created to bring glory to God in every part of our lives. Whether we're singing in church, working in our jobs, or serving others, our lives can be an offering of worship to the One who made us.

Worship also shifts our perspective. When we worship, we lift our eyes from our circumstances to the One who reigns over them. Psalm 121:1-2 declares, "I lift up my eyes to the mountains—where does my help come from? My help comes from the Lord, the Maker of heaven and earth." Worship reminds us that no problem is bigger than our God, no mountain too tall for Him to move. It replaces fear with faith and worry with wonder.

Finally, we worship because it connects us with heaven. Every time we worship, we join the eternal song of the angels, who cry out day and night,

"Holy, holy, holy is the Lord God Almighty, who was, and is, and is to come" (Revelation 4:8). Our worship here on earth is a glimpse of what we will do forever in heaven. It's a rehearsal for the day when we will stand before His throne, surrounded by the saints and the heavenly host, singing His praises for all eternity.

Worship is not just for Sundays. It's not confined to a building or a set time. Worship is a lifestyle—a continual outpouring of our love, gratitude, and adoration for the God who is worthy of it all. So why do we worship God? Because He is our Creator, our Savior, and our Sustainer. Because He is holy, loving, and good. Because He is worthy.

As you reflect on your own journey of worship, I encourage you to ask yourself: "Why do I worship God?" Let that question draw you closer to His heart and deepen your understanding of the One

The Power of Worship

you worship. May your worship be a wellspring of joy, a declaration of faith, and a reminder that He alone is worthy of all glory, honor, and praise.

Chapter 11

Worship That Echoes in Eternity

*They shall see His face, and His
name shall be on their foreheads.*

Revelation 22:4

As we draw this book to a close, I want to speak to you from my heart to yours. Worship is the one act that transcends time and space. It is the bridge that connects the earthly to the divine, the temporary to the eternal. As we live lives of worship here on earth, we are rehearsing for the ultimate worship experience in heaven—a place where worship never ceases and where God's glory radiates in unimaginable splendour.

Revelation 21:11 describes the New Jerusalem as having "the glory of God, its radiance like a most rare jewel, like jasper, clear as crystal." Imagine it: a city so magnificent that its foundation is adorned with every kind of precious stone. Revelation 21:19-20 lists these stones—jasper, sapphire, emerald, and amethyst, to name a few. These are not merely decorative; they are symbolic of God's creative power, His majesty, and the eternal beauty of His kingdom.

Picture the sea of glass mentioned in Revelation 4:6: "Before the throne there was as it were a sea of glass, like crystal." This isn't an ordinary sea; it represents the purity and stillness of God's presence. It reflects His holiness and reminds us that in heaven, there is no chaos, no turbulence—only perfect peace. Can you see it in your mind's eye? The saints, gathered before this sea, their voices blending in perfect harmony, singing, "Holy, holy, holy is the Lord God Almighty, who was, and is, and is to come" (Revelation 4:8).

In heaven, worship will be our eternal occupation. Revelation 5:11-13 gives us a glimpse: "Then I looked and heard the voice of many angels, numbering thousands upon thousands, and ten thousand times ten thousand. They encircled the throne and the living creatures and the elders. In a loud voice they were saying: 'Worthy is the Lamb, who was slain, to receive power and wealth and wisdom and strength and honor and glory and praise!'" The sound of this worship will be unlike anything we've ever experienced—a symphony of praise, echoing through eternity.

What a day it will be when we stand face-to-face with our Creator! Revelation 22:4 tells us, "They will see His face, and His name will be on their foreheads." In that moment, every tear will be wiped away, every sorrow will vanish, and we will bask in the glory of God's presence forever. The worship we experience here—through song, prayer, and surrender—is just a foretaste of the heavenly worship awaiting us.

Let me share this with you: the magnificence of heaven is not just in its beauty but in its focus. In heaven, the focus is not on the streets of gold or the gates of pearl, though they are awe-inspiring. The focus is on the Lamb of God, seated on the throne. Heaven's magnificence is in the unending worship of Jesus Christ, the One who redeemed us with His blood, the One who welcomes us into eternal glory.

But here's the incredible truth: we don't have to wait until heaven to experience this. When we worship here on earth, we catch glimpses of heaven.

Dr. Letitia McPherson

In those moments of worship when God's presence feels so near, it's as if the veil between heaven and earth is pulled back just a little. Worship allows us to taste the eternal even while we are bound by time.

As we reflect on the magnificence of heaven, let it fuel our worship now. Let the thought of streets of gold, the sea of glass, and the throne of God inspire us to live lives of worship that echo into eternity. Every time we bow our hearts in reverence, lift our voices in praise, or surrender our will to His, we are aligning ourselves with the eternal worship of heaven.

Dear Reader, as we end this chapter, I urge you to let the glories of heaven ignite your worship here on earth. Let the thought of standing before the throne of God, in the company of angels and saints, fill you with awe and anticipation. And as you worship today, remember that you are joining a heavenly chorus—a chorus that will never end.

"Now to Him who is able to do immeasurably more than all we ask or imagine, according to His power that is at work within us, to Him be glory in the church and in Christ Jesus throughout all generations, forever and ever! Amen" (Ephesians 3:20-21).

Conclusion

As we close the pages of this book, I want to leave you with a heartfelt invitation to make worship the rhythm of your life. Worship is more than songs, rituals, or fleeting moments—it is the very breath of our relationship with God, the anthem of our faith, and the vessel through which His presence flows into our lives.

Throughout this journey, we have explored the many dimensions of worship: its power as a weapon, its role in guiding us through trials, the beauty of worship in the waiting, and the eternal song we are destined to sing. Through it all, one truth remains constant: worship transforms us. It takes us from the struggles of earth to the glory of heaven, from the mundane to the magnificent, from fear to unwavering faith. Worship aligns our hearts with heaven, allowing us to glimpse the majesty and love of the God we serve.

Dear reader, worship is not confined to a church service or a specific moment in time. It is the posture of a surrendered heart, the overflow of gratitude, and the declaration of God's worth in every aspect of life. Whether you are kneeling in a quiet room, singing in the car, or lifting your hands in a congregation, your worship moves heaven and changes earth.

I encourage you to let worship permeate every corner of your life—your prayers, your work, your relationships, and even your trials. Let it be the song that carries you through every season, the anchor that holds you steady in life's storms. Worship is not about perfection; it's about presence—God's presence transforming you from the inside out.

Remember, your worship is a part of a greater story. Every time you lift your voice in praise, you join a heavenly chorus, a song that echoes through eternity. One day, we will stand before His throne, surrounded by saints and angels, in awe of His glory. What a moment that will be! Revelation 7:9-10 paints a breathtaking picture: "After this I looked, and behold, a great multitude that no one could number, from every nation, from all tribes and peoples and languages, standing before the throne and before the Lamb, clothed in white robes, with palm branches in their hands, and crying out with a loud voice, 'Salvation belongs to our God who sits on the throne, and to the Lamb!'"

Until that day comes, let us worship with every breath, every heartbeat, and every fiber of our being. Let us live lives of worship that glorify Him, reflect His love, and draw others to His presence. For we serve a God who is worthy of all glory, honor, and praise.

May your worship never cease, and may it always reflect the greatness of the One who is forever worthy.

Thank you for taking this journey with me. My prayer for you is that your life will become a song of worship, a testimony to God's greatness, and a reflection of His love. May your worship not only transform your life but also inspire those around you to seek the One who is worthy of it all.

With love and blessings,
Dr. Letitia McPherson

Dr. Letitia McPherson

On sale on Amazon, Barns and Noble and at www.gracebookstore.com

By God's Grace I Stand

The Power of Forgiveness

The Power of Faith

The Power of Worship

From the Mouth of the Prophet

Facing the Storms of Life

Walking Through the Valley

The Potter, The Clay, the Process

Places to Find Me

The Power of Worship

Join my mailing list for news, contests and exclusive content

Email me - bygodsgrace@bygodsgraceistand.com.

Find me on Facebook - https://www.facebook.com/bishop.mcpherson *

https://www.facebook.com/godsgraceistand

Websites: https://www.bygodsgraceistand.com

https://www.gracebookstore.com

My author page - https://www.facebook.com/Autho.rmcpherson

https://www.amazon.ca *
https://www.amazon.ca - Kindle Edition.

Dr. Letitia McPherson

"I can safely say, on the authority of all that is revealed in the Word of God, that any man or woman on this earth who is bored and turned off by worship is not ready for heaven."

—A.W. Tozer

"I need to worship because without it I can forget that I have a big God beside me and live in fear. I need to worship because without it I can forget his calling and begin to live in a spirit of self-preoccupation. I need to worship because without it I lose a sense of wonder and gratitude and plod through life with blinders on. I need worship because my natural tendency is toward self-reliance and stubborn independence."

—John Ortberg

"Nothing teaches us about the preciousness of the Creator as much as when we learn the emptiness of everything else."

—Charles Spurgeon

"Next to the Word of God, music deserves the highest praise. The gift of language combined with the gift of song was given to man that he should proclaim the Word of God through music."

—Martin Luther

The Power of Worship

Who will deny that true religion consists, in a great measure, in vigorous and lively actings of the inclination and will of the soul, or the fervent exercises of the heart? That religion which God requires, and will accept, does not consist in weak, dull, and lifeless, wishes, raising us but a little above a state of indifference."

—Jonathan Edwards

"The worship to which we are called in our renewed state is far too important to be left to personal preferences, to whims, or to marketing strategies. It is the pleasing of God that is at the heart of worship. Therefore, our worship must be informed at every point by the Word of God as we seek God's own instructions for worship that is pleasing to Him."

—R.C. Sproul

Dr. Letitia McPherson

Prophetic. Prolific. Profound.

Bishop Dr. Letitia E. McPherson is a dynamic woman of God who has transcended denominational boundaries and carried the Gospel to nations far and wide. Known as "The Woman with a Word and a Testimony," she is a sought-after preacher and teacher, celebrated for her uncompromised delivery of God's Word and her ability to transform lives through divine truth.

Born in Kellits, Clarendon, Jamaica, Dr. McPherson emigrated to Toronto, Canada, in 1969, where she continues to reside. Her academic accomplishments include a Bachelor of Arts in

Pastoral Theology, a Master of Arts in Pastoral Counseling, and dual Doctor of Divinity degrees in Pastoral Counseling and Pulpit Communication & Expository Preaching. Her extensive academic and spiritual training have prepared her to lead and serve with excellence.

Dr. McPherson is the founder and overseer of **Restoration Evangelistic Ministries International** and **Citadel of Hope International Ministries.** She is a beloved speaker at conferences, conventions, revivals, crusades, and camp meetings. Her remarkable ability to restructure ministries and draft by-laws, constitutions, and policy manuals has earned her a reputation as a trusted visionary and strategist. Her mandate remains unwavering: *"Win the lost at any cost"* and empower the Body of Christ to rise as the Revolutionary Army God has destined it to be.

Dr. Letitia McPherson

With a ministry footprint spanning four continents—Australia, Africa, North America, and Europe—and the Caribbean, Dr. McPherson's evangelistic zeal has touched countless lives. She is also a prolific author, with works including *The Potter, The Clay, The Process; Facing the Storms of Life; From the Mouth of the Prophet; Walking Through the Valley;* and her *Power Series* (*The Power of Forgiveness, The Power of Faith, The Power of Prayer, the Power of Worship and the Power of God's Grace*). Her memoir, *By God's Grace I Stand,* chronicles her extraordinary life and unwavering faith.

A testament to God's miraculous power, Dr. McPherson has overcome staggering health challenges, including eight major surgeries, five heart attacks, and 13 strokes. Most recently, she underwent her ninth surgery in 2020—a carotid artery procedure that marked another chapter in her incredible journey of faith and healing. Despite her personal trials, including the loss of her beloved husband of 26 years, Rev. Dr. Paul McPherson, she continues to stand as a beacon of hope and resilience, declaring the faithfulness of God.

Dr. McPherson's life mission is to *"Embrace the Globe with the Gospel of Jesus Christ."* She tirelessly travels to fulfill this call, carrying a timely word of truth, wisdom, and knowledge that empowers individuals and propels the Church into its divine destiny.

Above all, she treasures her roles as a mother to her three children—Paula, David, and Chris—and a grandmother to six precious grandchildren: Napthali, Latitia, Amara, David III, Azalea, and Rosabella. Her personal motto, *"By God's Grace I Stand,"* continues to inspire her life and ministry.

NOTES

The Power of Worship

Dr. Letitia McPherson

The Power of Worship

Dr. Letitia McPherson

The Power of Worship

www.ingramcontent.com/pod-product-compliance
Lightning Source LLC
Chambersburg PA
CBHW050555160426
43199CB00015B/2663